I0413498

MISSION

License and regulate the Nation's civilian use of byproduct, source, and special nuclear materials to ensure adequate protection of public health and safety, promote the common defense and security, and protect the environment.

TABLE OF CONTENTS

Commissioner Gregory B. Jaczko, Chairman Dale E. Klein,
and Commissioner Peter B. Lyons.

My fellow Commissioners and I are pleased to present the U.S. Nuclear Regulatory Commission's (NRC's) Strategic Plan for Fiscal Years 2008–2013. During this time period the agency will face significant changes and challenges, including the potential receipt of applications to construct and operate new nuclear power plants and to dispose of high-level radioactive waste. This updated Strategic Plan sets forth a broad vision of how the NRC will address these challenges.

As the agency prepares for these new responsibilities, our priority remains, as always, the adequate protection of public health, safety, and the environment, and promoting common defense and security. The NRC's Safety and Security strategic goals, as well as their associated strategic outcomes, continue to describe the agency's core functions and also remain essentially unchanged. This focus on safety and security ensures that the NRC remains a strong, independent, stable, and predictable regulator. The Strategic Plan also describes the agency's Organizational Excellence Objectives of Openness, Effectiveness, and Operational Excellence. These objectives characterize the manner in which the agency intends to achieve its Safety and Security goals.

In developing our Strategic Plan, the Commission benefited from input from our staff and external stakeholders, including members of the public, the Congress, and the nuclear industry. We thank all the stakeholders who shaped the Strategic Plan, as well as the NRC staff who worked diligently to produce a Strategic Plan that the Commission believes is comprehensive and clear. The Strategic Plan for Fiscal Years 2008–2013 will serve as a guide for how the NRC discharges its responsibilities to the American people.

About the NRC

The U.S. Nuclear Regulatory Commission (NRC or agency) was established by the Energy Reorganization Act of 1974 and began operations in 1975. The NRC was established to regulate the civilian use of nuclear materials for commercial, industrial, academic, and medical uses in order to protect public health and safety and the environment, and promote the common defense and security.

The NRC's scope of responsibility includes regulation of commercial nuclear power plants; research and test reactors; nuclear fuel cycle facilities; medical, academic, and industrial uses of radioactive materials; the decommissioning of these facilities and sites; and the transport, storage, and disposal of radioactive materials and wastes. The NRC's regulations are designed to protect both the public and occupational workers from radiation hazards.

The NRC is headed by five Commissioners appointed by the President of the United States, with the advice and consent of the U.S. Senate, to serve 5-year terms. The President designates one of the Commissioners to serve as Chairman. Under the leadership and policy direction of the Chairman and Commissioners, the NRC issues licenses and oversees licensees for civilian uses of radioactive materials, including 104 commercial nuclear power reactors; 33 research and test reactors; approximately 4,500 licensed reactor operators; 3 early site permits; 4 reactor design certifications; 40 uranium recovery sites; 9 major fuel cycle facilities; approximately 4,400 research, medical, industrial, government, and academic materials licensees; and an increasing number of independent spent fuel storage installations (currently 46 licensees). The NRC also consults with the U.S. Department of Energy (DOE) regarding disposal options for waste incidental to reprocessing and monitors DOE disposal actions for these incidental wastes.

The NRC is responsible for regulating domestic activities related to radiation protection and nuclear safety for nuclear facilities and for promoting the common defense and security related to uses of radioactive materials. The NRC also licenses the import and export of radioactive materials, participates in international nuclear activities, including multilateral and bilateral safety and security activities, and works closely with its international counterparts to enhance nuclear safety and security worldwide.

In addition, 34 States have signed agreements with the NRC under which they assume regulatory responsibility for the use of certain quantities of radioactive materials for civilian purposes in their respective States. These Agreement States implement State regulations that are compatible with NRC regulations. In all, they issue about 80 percent (17,600) of the more than 22,000 radioactive materials licensees in the United States. The NRC works closely with Agreement States to ensure a consistent regulatory framework, nationwide.

A Stable Regulator in a Dynamic Environment

The regulatory environment associated with the use of radioactive materials is changing. The expected receipt of applications to construct and operate new nuclear power plants, and to dispose of high-level radioactive waste, are two of the major challenges potentially facing the NRC over the next several years.

To meet these challenges, the NRC must efficiently use its resources, update the agency's regulatory review and construction inspection guidelines, and provide adequate infrastructure to accommodate staff.

Even as the NRC works to address growth in the industry, the agency's mission and values remain unchanged. The NRC's priority continues to be ensuring the adequate protection of public health, safety, and the environment, while promoting the common defense and security.

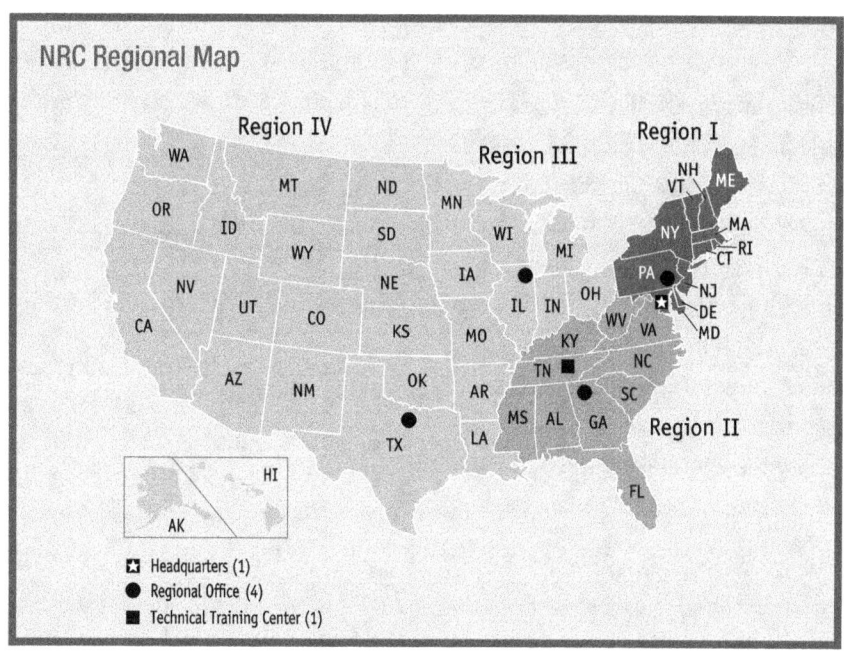

NRC Regional Map

Region IV
Region III
Region I
Region II

Headquarters (1)
Regional Office (4)
Technical Training Center (1)

Safety and security remain the agency's core functions, and the goals and strategic outcomes of the Strategic Plan are based on these functions. This focus on safety and security ensures that the NRC remains a strong, independent, stable, and predictable regulator.

Over the strategic planning period, the Nation is likely to see the following occur:

- The NRC expects to receive additional applications from entities that want to build and operate new nuclear power plants. The NRC also expects to receive applications for new fuel cycle facilities, including a significant number of uranium recovery applications.

- The DOE may submit an application to construct a high-level radioactive waste repository at Yucca Mountain, Nevada.

- Increasing quantities of spent nuclear fuel will be held in interim storage at reactor sites or transported to centralized interim storage sites awaiting permanent disposal.

- The NRC will continue to coordinate with a wide array of Federal, State, local, and Tribal authorities on issues related to license renewal, new reactor licensing, homeland security, emergency planning, and protection of the environment.

- The number of Agreement States will increase, as will the numbers of medical, academic, and industrial entities using radioactive materials under the oversight of the Agreement States.

The NRC recognizes that these changes will create an even greater need for effective and open communication with public stakeholders about a variety of issues. These include the safety and security of existing and proposed nuclear power plants and other licensed facilities and materials, emergency preparedness, and the impact on public health and safety and the environment from medical, academic, and industrial uses of licensed materials.

The unfolding of these complex regulatory issues also will require much more sophisticated techniques for the flow of documents and information, a process called knowledge management. The agency is in the process of attracting additional staff. We realize that in order to retain these highly skilled and educated professionals, who are critical to the agency, we must provide them the necessary resources to do their jobs effectively and a high degree of workplace satisfaction. The agency's comprehensive knowledge management approach is focused on ensuring that all staff members are highly trained in the technical disciplines relating to their duties, the regulatory processes that govern agency actions, and the regulatory principles inherent in making the agency a strong, independent, stable, and predictable regulator.

Being a stable and predictable regulator implies having effective and structured regulatory processes in place and ensuring that these processes are followed. New regulatory initiatives will be developed in accordance with these processes, open to public review and comment. The NRC is committed to considering and being responsive to stakeholder input before implementing any new regulatory initiative.

Organization of the Strategic Plan

This Plan describes the NRC's mission, values, and strategic goals of Safety and Security. For each of these goals, the Plan describes its strategic outcomes and discusses issues, strategies, and the means to support the strategies during this strategic planning period. The Plan then describes the organizational excellence objectives (i.e., openness, effectiveness, and operational excellence) to support the strategic goals of Safety and Security. For each of the excellence objectives, the Plan discusses issues and strategies.

Appendix A expands the discussion of the agency's strategic goals by noting key external factors that could affect the agency's ability to effectively execute this Strategic Plan.

Appendix B describes the schedule of planned program evaluations that the agency will use to adjust and refine its performance.

Appendix C is a glossary of terms used in the plan.

Key Elements in the Plan

Mission

License and regulate the Nation's civilian use of byproduct, source, and special nuclear materials to ensure adequate protection of public health and safety, promote the common defense and security, and protect the environment.

Values

The safe use of radioactive materials and nuclear fuels for beneficial civilian purposes is enabled by the agency's adherence to the principles of good regulation–independence, openness, efficiency, clarity, and reliability. In addition, regulatory actions are effective, realistic, and timely.

Strategic Goals

Safety: Ensure adequate protection of public health and safety and the environment.

Security: Ensure adequate protection in the secure use and management of radioactive materials.

Refueling a nuclear reactor.

Goal:
Ensure adequate protection of public health and safety and the environment.

Strategic Outcomes

- Prevent the occurrence of any nuclear reactor accidents.

- Prevent the occurrence of any inadvertent criticality events.

- Prevent the occurrence of any acute radiation exposures resulting in fatalities.

- Prevent the occurrence of any releases of radioactive materials that result in significant radiation exposures.

- Prevent the occurrence of any releases of radioactive materials that cause significant adverse environmental impacts.

Discussion

The NRC's primary function is to regulate the safe use of radioactive materials for civilian purposes to ensure adequate protection of public health and safety and the environment. In responding to anticipated developments in the nuclear arena over the next several years, including the review of a number of new nuclear reactor applications, the NRC will continue to place significant emphasis on strengthening the interrelationship among safety, security, and emergency preparedness.

The NRC achieves its Safety goal by licensing individuals and organizations to use radioactive materials for beneficial civilian purposes and then ensuring that these licensees perform at acceptable safety levels. In particular, the agency maintains vigilance over safety performance through licensing reviews, inspections, expanded oversight (when needed), rulemaking, and incident response. The NRC continually seeks to identify and resolve potential safety issues, including those with generic implications for multiple reactors and licensees. The NRC also uses enforcement actions to require licensees to correct license deficiencies. These include issuing orders for corrective action, issuing shutdown orders, imposing civil penalties, seeking criminal prosecution, or suspending or revoking a license.

The agency's regulatory activities are consistent with the risk presented by specific uses, incorporating sound science and operating experience to ensure that licensees have adequate safety margins. In carrying out its safety mission, the NRC employs the full range of actions necessary to ensure that a licensee's performance does not fall below acceptable levels.

Important current and future challenges for the agency include materials degradation issues at existing nuclear power plants; high-level waste transport, storage, and disposal; new and evolving technologies, including digital instrumentation and controls; and analyzing domestic and international operating experience and other events of national interest for lessons learned and best practices. Other considerations include upgrading incident response systems, employing a multifaceted regulatory approach, and cooperating and coordinating with other domestic agencies and government entities.

About half of the operating nuclear power plants in the United States have received 20-year extensions of their operating licenses, and most of the rest are expected to apply for license extensions in the future. Materials degradation is the primary consideration in

NRC inspector examining reaction levels at a nuclear power plant.

granting a license extension. The aim of the license renewal process is to evaluate whether aging effects are monitored, managed, and controlled such that safety is ensured for the renewal period. License renewal applications for aging plants call for analysis of the robustness, longevity, and continued performance of nuclear power plant components, such as electric cabling, piping, and containment structures.

Nuclear facility licensees are replacing analog instrumentation and control equipment with digital equipment because analog replacement parts are becoming more difficult to obtain. Digital systems also offer potentially better performance and features than analog systems. New advanced reactor plants are expected to use advanced digital instrumentation and control systems and control room operator interfaces, presenting regulatory and licensing challenges for the agency and the nuclear industry.

The agency is preparing for the review of applications to construct and operate a new generation of nuclear plants. The agency has reorganized its headquarters reactor licensing organization to dedicate the necessary resources to conduct timely reviews of these applications while also ensuring that adequate resources are available to support the operational safety of the current fleet of reactors.

With the development of new reactor designs and other new facilities and technologies, the NRC is working closely with regulators in other countries interested in participating in the Multinational Design Evaluation Program, in which several nations jointly cooperate in sharing information regarding the review of new reactor designs. These next-generation designs require detailed evaluation of their vulnerability to accidents and attacks, as well as development of inspections, tests, analyses, and acceptance criteria for their construction. First-of-a-kind construction, startup, and operation of several U.S.-designed nuclear power plants will continue to occur outside of the United States. A significant percentage of the major components both for these initial plants and for plants that may eventually be built in the United States will be manufactured in other countries. In response, the NRC is actively engaged with its counterpart regulatory authorities in these countries in enhancing the sharing of relevant information, experience, and expertise.

The agency is also preparing for the review of the DOE's anticipated application to establish the Nation's first repository for high-level radioactive waste at Yucca Mountain, Nevada. The NRC's review of this application will require evaluation of a wide range of technical and scientific analyses and the resolution of various regulatory issues on a challenging schedule. Additionally, the Nation will require the continued safe management of interim storage capacity for spent nuclear fuel. Toward that end, the NRC regulates various options for interim storage, including onsite spent fuel pools and dry casks at independent spent fuel storage installations in a risk-informed and performance-based manner consistent with the approach the NRC takes to regulating reactors. In addition, the NRC regulates the safety of spent fuel transportation packages. These packages are evaluated, tested, and certified as capable of safely transporting spent fuel from reactor sites or other storage facilities.

Industry interest in fuel cycle facilities is expected to continue, with these projects requiring NRC review. The staff expects to receive two new license applications for uranium enrichment plants. The agency is also reviewing applications for new uranium recovery sites, restarts, or expansions of existing facilities from U.S. corporations participating in the domestic and international uranium markets to support the new generation of nuclear plants. Furthermore, the NRC is reviewing a license application for a mixed-oxide fuel facility that would use plutonium salvaged from decommissioned nuclear weapons to fabricate fuel assemblies for use in nuclear power plants as a technique to reduce existing quantities of weapons-usable materials.

The NRC employs a multifaceted regulatory approach to meet the continuing challenge of insisting that its licensees operate nuclear facilities and use radioactive materials safely.

Additionally, the NRC believes that close cooperation among Federal agencies, State authorities, and local and Tribal authorities will lead to more effective regulation. Therefore, the NRC works with other Federal agencies, such as the Environmental Protection Agency, Occupational Safety and Health Administration, Food and Drug Administration, and the DOE, Transportation, Justice, and Homeland Security, as well as State, local, and Tribal authorities, to ensure appropriate coordination for the accomplishment of its mission. States that have entered into Agreements with the Commission carry out coordinated and comparable programs for nuclear materials within their borders.

Nuclear safety is a global issue and a continuing challenge. The NRC closely cooperates with its counterpart foreign regulatory bodies and international organizations, such as the International Atomic Energy Agency and the Organization for Economic Cooperation and Development's Nuclear Energy Agency, to share information, resources, best practices, and lessons learned from operating experience and to influence the development of standards and guidance consistent with U.S. objectives.

Safety Goal Strategies

1. Develop, maintain, and implement licensing and regulatory programs for reactors, fuel facilities, materials users, spent fuel management, uranium recovery, and decommissioning activities to ensure the adequate protection of public health and safety and the environment.

2. Continue to oversee the safe operation of existing plants while preparing for and managing the review of applications for new power reactors.

3. Conduct NRC safety, security, and emergency preparedness programs in an integrated manner.

4. Improve the NRC's regulatory programs and apply safety-focused research to anticipate and resolve safety issues.

5. Use sound science and state-of-the-art methods to establish, where appropriate, risk-informed and performance-based regulations.

6. Promote focused attention on safety matters and individual accountability of those engaged in regulated activities.

7. Use domestic and international operating experience to inform decisionmaking.

8. Oversee licensee safety performance through inspections, investigations, enforcement, and performance assessment activities.

9. Effectively respond to events at NRC-licensed facilities and other events of national interest, including maintaining and enhancing the NRC's critical incident response and communication capabilities.

Means to Support Safety Strategies

The NRC conducts a number of programs and initiatives to ensure adequate protection of public health and safety and the environment. The major programs include rulemaking, licensing, technical reviews and inspection, incident response and emergency preparedness, domestic and international information exchange and cooperation with the Agreement State program, and research programs. The NRC will conduct a number of programs and initiatives during this strategic planning period, including the following:

- Review licensing requests (e.g., new applications, amendments, renewals, terminations) to confirm that they provide an adequate margin of safety consistent with the agency's rules and regulations. Conduct environmental reviews as appropriate to ensure that actions comply with the National Environmental Policy Act of 1969. [Supports Strategies 1 and 2.]

- Implement, review, and refine the Reactor Oversight Process, the principal program for overseeing nuclear power plant operation, to better identify significant performance issues and to ensure that licensees take appropriate actions to maintain acceptable safety performance. [Supports Strategies 5 and 8.]

- Implement, review, and refine materials oversight. [Supports Strategy 8.]

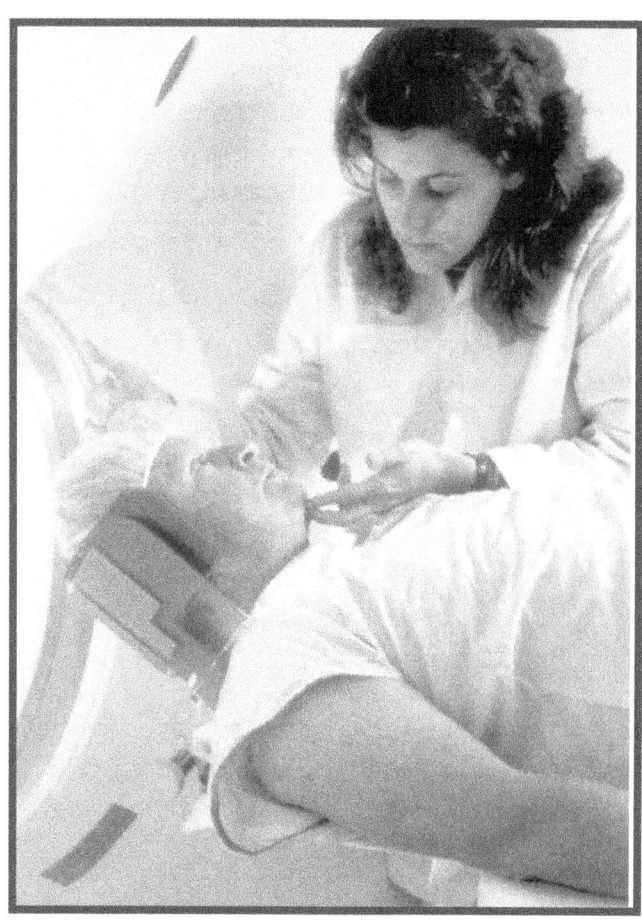

Patient prepared for Computerized Tomography (CT) Scan.

- Maintain qualified inspectors at nuclear power reactor and certain fuel cycle sites (resident inspectors), in the NRC's four regional offices (regional inspectors and license examiners), and at the agency's headquarters. [Supports Strategies 1, 6, and 8.]

- Maintain the readiness and capabilities of the NRC Headquarters Operations Center and Regional Response Centers, which coordinate and monitor the agency's response to incidents and reportable conditions and licensees' actions to ensure safety at their facilities. [Supports Strategies 3, 5, and 9.]

- Participate in emergency preparedness exercises that involve a wide array of Federal, State, local, and Tribal authorities and emergency response personnel, and use cooperative intergovernmental relationships to balance national response capabilities. [Supports Strategies 3, 6, and 9.]

- Conduct a program for the identification and resolution of reactor, fuel cycle, materials, and radioactive waste generic issues. [Supports Strategies 2, 3, and 4.]

- Establish and maintain stable and predictable regulatory programs and policies for all stakeholders. Verify that all new regulatory initiatives adhere to these programs and policies. [Supports Strategies 1, 2, and 6.]

- Maintain an open, collaborative working environment that encourages all employees and contractors to raise safety issues and differing views without fear of retaliation. [Supports Strategies 1, 3, and 5.]

- Maintain a safety framework of rules, regulatory guidance, and standard review plans that promotes licensee compliance with underlying safety principles and stakeholder understanding. [Supports Strategy 8.]

- Conduct research programs to identify, lead, and/or sponsor reviews that support the resolution of ongoing and future safety issues, including providing tools and expertise needed to support the NRC's independent decisionmaking process. [Supports Strategies 1, 2, 3, 4, and 5.]

- Conduct prelicensing consultation and begin review of the potential application for the Yucca Mountain repository when it is received. [Supports Strategies 1 and 2.]

- Complete technical reviews and inspections of new spent fuel dry storage systems and facilities for the safe and secure storage of spent fuel. Apply risk insights gained from spent fuel dry storage probabilistic risk assessment in these reviews and inspections in a manner consistent with the application of these insights in reactor regulation. [Supports Strategies 1 and 3.]

- Test a representative spent fuel transportation package design under transportation accident conditions to verify package performance and modeling capability. [Supports Strategies 1 and 5.]

- Conduct periodic reviews of Agreement State programs to ensure that they are adequate to protect public health and safety and the environment and are compatible with the NRC's program. [Supports Strategies 2, 3, and 6.]

- Work closely with the Agreement States to develop consistent, risk-informed processes to review event information and identify safety issues for materials licensees. [Supports Strategies 2, 3, and 6.]

- Use the information from integrated safety analyses implementing a graded approach to monitor and respond to activities at fuel fabrication facilities. Use the lessons learned from these analyses to develop more risk-informed oversight programs. [Supports Strategies 1 and 4.]

- Assess the key issues affecting the safe management of civilian low-level radioactive storage and waste disposal to facilitate planning so that potential disruption in access to the three licensed disposal sites does not adversely affect licensees' ability to operate and decommission their facilities safely. [Supports Strategies 1 and 6.]

■ Evaluate domestic and international operating events and trends for risk significance and generic applicability in order to improve NRC programs. [Supports Strategy 7.]

■ Work with international counterparts to exchange information, expertise, operating experiences, and ongoing research to recognize and respond to emerging technical issues and to promote best practices. Participate in the development and evaluation of international standards to ensure they are soundly based and determine whether substantial safety improvements can be identified and incorporated domestically. [Supports Strategies 5 and 7.]

■ Review and refine an enforcement framework that emphasizes the importance of compliance with regulatory requirements and encourages prompt identification and comprehensive correction of licensee violations. [Supports Strategy 8.]

The Director of NRC's Office of New Reactors accepts a Combined License application for the North Anna site in Virginia.

Goal:
Ensure adequate protection in the secure use and management of radioactive materials.

Strategic Outcome

■ Prevent any instances where licensed radioactive materials are used domestically in a manner hostile to the United States.

Discussion

The NRC must remain vigilant of the security of nuclear facilities and materials. The agency achieves its common defense and Security goal using licensing and oversight programs similar to those employed in achieving its safety goal. The aim is to allow licensees to realize the benefits of nuclear materials through their secure use, while at the same time placing only necessary regulatory requirements on those licensees.

The NRC also requires that licensees maintain controls over high-risk radiation sources and other risk-significant radioactive materials and successfully implement tracking and accounting systems. These systems help ensure that the radioactive materials used by licensees are stored and maintained securely.

Maintaining a stable and predictable security environment is one of the NRC's major continuing challenges. It requires ensuring adequate security without unduly limiting the beneficial use of radioactive materials. To attain this balance, the NRC must upgrade its infrastructure for protecting and sharing classified and safeguards information, and for sharing sensitive information, as appropriate, with licensees, members of the public, and other Federal, State, local, and Tribal authorities and international stakeholders.

Another major task is implementing the authorities granted to the NRC in the Energy Policy Act of 2005 for enhancing the security of nuclear facilities and radioactive material. The NRC is in the process of completing rulemakings and other actions recommended by the multiagency Task Force on Radiation Source Protection and Security, which was established by this Act. In August 2006, the Task Force issued its first report containing recommendations for improving the security of radioactive sources. Subsequent reports are due not less than once every 4 years.

The NRC also has completed the process of identifying vulnerabilities at licensed facilities and developing strategies to mitigate those vulnerabilities. The agency is now working with licensees to implement those strategies. The design-basis threat is used to assess the level of threat against which licensees must realistically be expected to defend with high assurance.

The NRC also currently maintains its role in international activities related to the security of radioactive materials and facilities, including (1) contributing to the formulation of foreign policy guidance, (2) providing international assistance in nuclear security, material control and accounting, and safeguards, (3) reviewing applications and issuing import and export licenses for nuclear materials and equipment, and (4) cooperating with the International Atomic Energy Agency and the Organization for Economic Cooperation and Development's Nuclear Energy Agency on nuclear safeguards, nonproliferation, and international regulatory standards.

Security Goal Strategies

1. Use relevant intelligence information and security assessments to maintain realistic and effective security requirements and mitigation measures.

2. Share security information with appropriate stakeholders and international partners.

3. Oversee licensee security performance through inspections and force-on-force exercises.

4. Control the handling and storage of sensitive security information and the communication of information to licensees and Federal, State, and local partners.

5. Support Federal response plans that employ an approach to the security of nuclear facilities and radioactive material that integrates the efforts of licensees and Federal, State, local, and Tribal authorities.

6. Use a risk-informed approach to implement appropriate regulatory controls for the possession, handling, import, export, and transshipment of radioactive materials.

7. Enhance the programs to control of the security of radioactive sources and strategic special nuclear materials commensurate with their risk, including enhancements required by the Energy Policy Act of 2005.

8. Promote U.S. national security interests and nuclear nonproliferation policy objectives for NRC-licensed imports and exports of source and special nuclear materials and nuclear equipment.

Means to Support Security Strategies

To maintain the secure use and management of radioactive materials, the NRC conducts a number of programs and initiatives, including the following:

■ Assess the threat environment to maintain an adequate regulatory framework, using new information from domestic research and cooperative research programs with international partners. [Supports Strategies 1, 4, 5, 6, and 8.]

■ Conduct inspections to assess licensees' security performance. The NRC will conduct followup reviews, inspections, or investigations as needed when security problems are identified. [Supports Strategies 2, 3, and 6.]

■ On a 3-year cycle, conduct security performance evaluations at each applicable nuclear facility to assess each licensee's protective strategy capabilities and to evaluate support functions provided by Federal, State, and local law enforcement and emergency planning officials for each licensee. [Supports Strategies 1, 3, 4, and 5.]

■ As necessary, conduct security assessments and determine the consequences of a range of threats against existing safety, safeguards, and security requirements. The NRC will share the results with Federal partners to support an integrated national posture for protecting of the Nation's critical infrastructure. [Supports Strategies 1, 4, and 5.]

■ Work with the Homeland Security Council, the Department of Homeland Security, and the intelligence community to define, develop, and implement integrated security response plans and

NRC Operations Center during an emergency planning exercise.

the National Response Plan, which incorporates Federal, State, local, and Tribal government assets. [Supports Strategies 4, 5, and 8.]

■ Work with States on safety and security measures related to NRC- and State-licensed facilities and activities within their borders. [Supports Strategies 4 and 5.]

■ Collaborate with the DOE, Department of Homeland Security, and other agencies and State governments to develop and implement a national registry of radioactive sources. Improve the controls on high-risk radioactive materials, including enhancements required by the Energy Policy Act of 2005 and recommended by the Task Force on Radiation Source Protection and Security, to prevent their harmful use. [Supports Strategies 1, 4, 6, and 7.]

■ Continue to support and participate in international security activities, including support of International Atomic Energy Agency nonproliferation initiatives and bilateral physical security initiatives undertaken with countries that receive special nuclear materials and equipment from the United States. [Supports Strategy 8.]

■ Identify and obtain access to critical electronic channels of security information maintained by other Federal agencies to ensure that the NRC and its licensees maintain a current awareness of potential threats to licensed facilities and activities. [Supports Strategies 1 and 4.]

■ Identify and develop key information technology investments, including secure electronic document and records management capabilities, that will enhance the storage, handling, and communication of sensitive security information both within and external to the agency. [Supports Strategy 4.]

The Director of NRC's Office of Nuclear Security and Incident Response discusses homeland security strategy.

■ Support U.S. Government goals to secure nuclear materials internationally through bilateral agreements to support material control and accounting programs. [Supports Strategies 2, 7, and 8.]

South Texas Nuclear Generating Station, southwest of Bay City, Texas.

Objectives:

- **Openness**
- **Effectiveness**
- **Operational Excellence**

OPENNESS

The NRC appropriately informs and involves stakeholders in the regulatory process.

Discussion

The NRC views nuclear regulation as the public's business and, as such, believes it should be transacted as openly and candidly as possible to maintain and enhance the public's confidence. Ensuring appropriate openness explicitly recognizes that the public must be informed about, and have a reasonable opportunity to participate meaningfully in, the NRC's regulatory processes. At the same time the NRC must also control sensitive information so that security goals are met.

NRC engineer is the focus of a Spanish-language interview on the nuclear licensing process.

Over the next several years, the NRC anticipates receiving license applications for the construction and operation of a number of nuclear power plants, nuclear materials facilities, and a geologic repository. In addition, the NRC expects an increase in the number of spent fuel shipments and applications to extend the licenses of operating reactors. These activities will generate a great deal of public interest. Stakeholders will have many opportunities to participate in the regulatory process before issuance of a license, construction permit, early site permit, design certification, or combined license. For this participation to be meaningful, stakeholders must have access to clear and understandable information about the NRC's role, processes, activities, and decisionmaking. The NRC will engage in active communications with stakeholders to ensure mutual understanding and timely response.

To continue its practice of communicating clearly and frequently on operating plant and materials activities, the NRC will hold meetings with the public or other external stakeholders both in the vicinity of nuclear facilities and at its headquarters and regional offices. In addition, documents and correspondence related to license renewals, license applications, and inspection findings, with the exception of certain security-related, proprietary, and other sensitive information, are made available through the agency's public Web site at http://www.nrc.gov. The agency issues press releases when it receives license applications and announces public meetings, opportunities for hearings, and other avenues for public involvement. Copies of key documents and notifications are sent to Federal, State, local, and Tribal authorities; published in the *Federal Register*; and made available electronically on the NRC Web site. Librarians at the NRC's Public Document Room are available to assist members of the public in accessing or obtaining copies of the agency's public documents. To complement the agency's public outreach activities, the NRC has an established process to respond to requests made under the Freedom of Information Act.

Openness Strategies

1. Enhance awareness of the NRC's independent role in protecting public health and safety, the environment, and the common defense and security.

2. Provide accurate and timely information to the public about the NRC's mission, regulatory activities, and performance and about the uses of, and risks associated with, radioactive materials.

3. Provide for fair, timely, and meaningful stakeholder involvement in NRC decisionmaking without disclosing classified, safeguards, proprietary, and sensitive unclassified information.

4. Communicate about the NRC's role, processes, activities, and decisions in plain language that is clear and understandable to the public.

5. Initiate early communication with stakeholders on issues of substantial interest.

EFFECTIVENESS

NRC actions are high quality, efficient, timely, and realistic, to enable the safe and beneficial use of radioactive materials.

Discussion

The NRC anticipates a significant increase in agency workload over the next several years. The increase is coming at a time when initiatives such as the Government Performance and Results Act (GPRA) continue to challenge Federal agencies to become more effective and efficient and to justify their budget requests with demonstrated program results.

The concept of effectiveness applies to all levels of the agency, from individual actions to programs and agencywide initiatives. At the program level, for example, effectiveness refers to the degree of success in achieving program goals and requires careful alignment with intended program results to ensure

Public meeting in Mississippi on the Grand Gulf early site permit application.

that the right work is being performed by the right people. With respect to the next generation of nuclear reactors, effectiveness refers to the scope and technical sufficiency of the application review. The NRC's ability to conduct effective application reviews relies on a variety of strategies and activities, described below.

Efficiency refers to timeliness, productivity, quality, and cost characteristics that together define how economically an activity or process is performed. The NRC recognizes that the efficiency of the agency's regulatory processes is important to the regulated community and other stakeholders, including Federal, State, local, and Tribal authorities and the public. The timeliness of the application review can be increased without compromising safety and security, provided industry submits complete, high-quality applications.

While the NRC will never compromise safety and security for increased efficiency, the agency works to improve the efficiency of its regulatory processes wherever possible.

Effectiveness Strategies

1. Use state-of-the-art technologies and risk insights to improve the effectiveness and realism of NRC actions, with a goal of continuous improvement.

2. Provide clear and timely guidance to applicants and licensees to foster the submittal of high-quality and timely applications or license amendment requests.

3. Reach high-quality and timely decisions.

4. Cooperate with Federal agencies, States, and Tribal authorities and international counterparts to gain insights and effectively resolve issues to enable the safe and beneficial use of radioactive materials.

5. Work with stakeholders to minimize regulatory or jurisdictional overlap.

6. Anticipate challenges and promptly evaluate and respond to changes in the regulatory and technical environment.

7. Continue to improve the NRC's regulatory and communication programs.

8. Achieve efficiencies in the licensing process that enable the safe and secure use of nuclear material.

OPERATIONAL EXCELLENCE

NRC operations use effective business methods and solutions to achieve excellence in accomplishing the agency's mission.

Discussion

The NRC works to achieve operational excellence in all agency programs and processes. Operational excellence is primarily achieved through effective leadership in providing timely, high-quality information management and information technology; hiring and retaining knowledgeable and skilled staff; and providing accurate and timely financial information.

Timely, high-quality information is critical to the achievement of the NRC's safety and security mission.

The NRC's information technology/information management systems and services must work effectively to deliver that information to all participants in the regulatory process, including internal and external stakeholders. In addition, information technology continues to offer significant opportunities for improving the efficiency and effectiveness of NRC operations. For additional information, see the NRC Information Technology/Information Management Strategic Plan, available at http://www.nrc.gov.

The NRC's workforce possesses detailed knowledge and specialized technical skills that enable the agency to fulfill its mission. To maintain this expertise and respond to emerging needs, the NRC will need to continue to build its human capital in diverse areas. The individuals hired with these skills will achieve their greatest effectiveness when they are appropriately deployed, fully engaged in fulfilling the NRC's mission requirements, provided appropriate training as needed, and recognized for their performance. The NRC is dedicated to maintaining its technical excellence and regulatory process proficiency now and in the future through a strategic approach to training, development, and knowledge management. As the agency evolves its knowledge management program into the future, the program will adopt a comprehensive, integrated lifecycle approach to organizational learning and knowledge management. For additional information, see the NRC Strategic Human Capital Plan, available at http://www.nrc.gov.

Accurate and timely financial information is another component of operational excellence and is critical to enabling agency managers to achieve the NRC's safety and security goals while efficiently using resources. Quality financial information enhances the effectiveness of agency managerial decisions and has the potential to reduce the fees borne by licensees, as well as the public's tax burden.

Chairman Dale E. Klein at the ceremony to recognize NRC as the 2007 Best Place to Work in the Federal Government.

Operational Excellence Strategies

1. Strengthen accountability for setting and achieving individual and organizational performance expectations and for providing timely and comprehensive feedback.

2. Reward safety-conscious actions and improve communication throughout the organization to support a culture of openness, trust, and innovation.

3. Improve support services to make them more efficient and make it easier to accomplish agency goals.

4. Manage agency information and employ information technology to improve the productivity, effectiveness, and efficiency of agency programs and enhance the availability and usefulness of information to all users inside and outside the agency.

5. Use innovative strategies to recruit, develop, and retain a high-quality, diverse workforce.

6. Continue to foster a work environment that is free of discrimination and provides maximum opportunities for all employees to use their diverse talents in support of the NRC's mission and goals.

7. Sustain a learning environment that provides continuing improvement in performance through knowledge management, performance feedback, training, coaching, and mentoring.

8. Ensure that the NRC has the appropriate physical facilities to ensure regulatory effectiveness and operational efficiency.

9. Provide accurate, timely, and useful financial information to agency managers for effective decisionmaking.

APPENDIX A: KEY EXTERNAL FACTORS

The NRC's ability to achieve its goals depends on a changing mix of industry operating experience, national priorities, market forces, and availability of resources. A process for managing change should continue to be refined and implemented to ensure that the NRC is ready to address changing priorities in a timely manner. This appendix discusses significant external factors, all of which are beyond the control of the NRC but could have an impact on the agency's ability to achieve its strategic goals.

Receipt of New Reactor License Applications

A resurgence of interest in new nuclear power plants is leading to intense competition for qualified individuals to serve as technical staff for both the NRC and its licensees and as nuclear power plant operating personnel. Increasing turnover and competition for qualified staff, as well as the loss of expertise as older members of the workforce retire, will remain an NRC challenge for the next several years.

Significant Operating Incident (Domestic or International)

A significant incident at a licensed nuclear facility could cause the agency to reassess its safety and security requirements, which could change the agency's focus on some initiatives related to its goals until the situation stabilizes. Because the NRC's stakeholders (including the public) are highly sensitive to many issues regarding the use of radioactive materials, events of relatively minor safety or security significance could potentially require a response that consumes considerable agency resources.

Significant Terrorist Incident

A significant terrorist incident anywhere in the United States would heighten the NRC's oversight and response stance. Subsequent new or changed security requirements or other policy decisions might affect the NRC, its partners, and the industry it regulates. A significant terrorist incident at a nuclear facility or activity anywhere in the world that departs from the agency's evaluation of threat parameters could result in impacts on the NRC's priorities and potentially in U.S. policy regarding export activities, the NRC's role in international security, and/or requirements for security at U.S. nuclear power plants and other licensee facilities.

Emergency Preparedness and Incident Response

Emergency preparedness and incident response activities with Federal, State, local, and Tribal authorities continue to increase in scope and number. This affects the agency's priorities and workloads.

Timing of a Department of Energy Application for the High-Level Waste Repository at Yucca Mountain and Related Activities

The licensing of the proposed repository for spent nuclear fuel represents a major effort for the NRC in planning, review, analysis, and ultimate decisionmaking. DOE has indicated that it intends to submit a license application for a high-level waste repository by June 2008. The timing of the DOE actions will heavily influence the NRC's resource allocation decisions over the next several years. Acceleration or delay in the DOE activities may affect other programs that are directly associated with achieving the agency's goals.

Legislative Initiatives

Legislative initiatives under consideration by the Congress can have a major impact on the NRC. For example, the Energy Policy Act of 2005 has greatly affected the agency's priorities and workload. Increasing interest in diversified sources of energy and energy independence is leading to an expected increase in license applications for nuclear power plants. The attendant increase in resources devoted to license review and analysis is affecting how the agency goes about achieving its goals for this planning period.

Advanced Fuel Cycle Development

The Global Nuclear Energy Partnership has been proposed by the DOE as a means to recycle (reprocess) nuclear fuel using proliferation-resistant technologies to recover more energy and reduce waste. The impacts on the NRC could include developing the licensing requirements for, and then licensing, commercial reprocessing facilities, advanced burner reactors, and associated storage and waste facilities. The scope and schedule of NRC activities are uncertain.

APPENDIX B: PLANNED PROGRAM EVALUATIONS

Operator Licensing Program

Expected Completion Dates: FY 2008, FY 2009, FY 2010, FY 2011, FY 2012, FY 2013

Objective: The annual evaluation of the Operator Licensing Program ensures that the program is effective and consistently implements the requirements in 10 CFR Part 55, the guidance in NUREG-1021, "Operator Licensing Examination Standards for Power Reactors," and other policy documents.

Scope: The annual evaluation of the Operator Licensing Program audits one or two written examinations and operating tests in each Region to ensure consistent quality, level of difficulty, administration, and grading. The evaluation also includes a detailed review of the operator licensing function in two regional offices each year, with each region performing a similar self-assessment during the alternate years. The detailed reviews assess seven functional areas, including administrative requirements, written examinations, operating tests, requalification program oversight, regional operations, licensing assistant activities, and resource utilization.

Reactor Oversight Program

Expected Completion Dates: FY 2008, FY 2009, FY 2010, FY 2011, FY 2012, FY 2013

Objectives: The annual Reactor Oversight Program evaluation has two objectives—(1) to determine whether the ongoing program is effective in supporting the achievement of the performance goals and the agency's Strategic Plan goals, and (2) to provide timely, objective information to inform program planning and improvements.

Scope: At minimum, the evaluation will include (1) the efficiency of the agency's baseline inspection program,

(2) the effectiveness of the significance determination process, (3) the usefulness of current performance indicators for enhancing agency planning and response, and (4) the effectiveness of the assessment program to prescribe appropriate regulatory oversight to those plants with performance deficiencies.

Management Work Planning Process

Expected Completion Date: FY 2008

Objective: The evaluation of the work planning process within the Office of Nuclear Reactor Regulation is intended to improve the effectiveness and efficiency of the planning process to better serve the office's workload management needs. The primary scope is to conduct an effectiveness review of the office's work planning process by (1) assessing the current services provided by the work planning center, (2) developing recommendations on adding, deleting or modifying current services aimed at improving the effectiveness and efficiency of the workload management services, (3) developing recommendations as to what processes should be included under the auspices of the centralized work planning program, and (4) developing recommended steps to improve the information technology systems that support the work planning process.

Scope: The project includes the evaluation of the work planning process; the evaluation is intended to improve the effectiveness and efficiency of the planning process to better serve the Office of Nuclear Reactor Regulation's workload management needs.

Integrated Materials Performance Evaluation Program Reviews of Selected NRC Regional Offices

Expected Completion Date: Region IV in FY 2009

Objective: Each Program Evaluation will determine whether the regional offices are conducting programs that meet the objectives set out in Management Directive 5.6, "Integrated Materials Performance Evaluation Program (IMPEP)."

Scope: The evaluations will include performance criteria (technical staffing and training, status of the Materials Inspection Program, technical quality of inspections, technical quality of licensing actions, and technical quality of responses to incidents and allegations) that are common to all regions as well as appropriate criteria for region-specific activities and responsibilities. The evaluation will be conducted in accordance with Management Directive 5.6 and the implementing procedures. The findings and report will be finalized after evaluation by the Management Review Board. Any recommendations or good practices will be factored into future activities for all of the regional materials programs.

Fuel Cycle Licensing and Inspection Program

Expected Completion Date: FY 2009

Objective: The fuel cycle licensing and inspection program provides regulatory oversight for fuel cycle facilities in the areas of safety, safeguards and environmental protection. Findings from previous Program Assessment Rating Tool reviews for the Fuel Cycle Licensing and Inspection Program were used to strengthen the alignment of program performance measures with the agency's strategic outcomes, as well as to better demonstrate contributions of program activities and outputs. Ongoing efforts are being implemented to develop independent assessments to validate and confirm that the program objectives are continuing to be met in an efficient and effective manner.

Scope: The effort will focus on independent reviews to assess and evaluate the effectiveness of the Fuel Cycle Licensing and Inspection Program.

APPENDIX C: GLOSSARY

Agreement State: a State that has signed an agreement with the NRC providing for the State to regulate the use of certain radioactive materials within its borders and the discontinuance of Federal authority in that State (does not apply to the regulation of operating commercial nuclear reactors).

Defense in Depth: an element of the NRC's Safety Philosophy that employs successive compensatory measures to prevent accidents or lessen the effects of damage if a malfunction or accident occurs at a nuclear facility. The NRC's safety philosophy ensures that the public is adequately protected and that emergency plans surrounding a nuclear facility are well conceived and will work. Moreover, the philosophy ensures that safety will not be wholly dependent on any single element of the design, construction, maintenance, or operation of a nuclear facility.

Design-Basis Threat: a profile of the type, composition, and capabilities of an adversary. The NRC and its licensees use the design-basis threat as a basis for designing safeguards systems to protect against acts of radiological sabotage and to prevent the theft of special nuclear materials.

Diversity Management: The goal of diversity management is to enable all employees to reach their full potential in pursuit of the organization's mission. This includes fostering an environment where diversity is commonplace and enhances execution of the agency's objectives.

Effectiveness: ability to achieve the intended outcome(s) of an activity, program, or process. A program cannot be considered effective if it is not meeting its objectives and achieving the intended outcome(s).

Efficiency: the ability to act with a minimum of waste, expense, or unnecessary effort. Efficiency embodies a combination of productivity, cost, timeliness, and quality.

High-Level Waste: the highly radioactive materials that are produced as byproducts of the reactions that occur inside nuclear reactors. Such wastes take one of two forms, becoming either spent (used) reactor fuel when it is accepted for disposal or waste materials that remain after spent fuel is reprocessed.

Low-Level Waste: items that have become contaminated with radioactive material or have become radioactive through exposure to neutron radiation. This waste typically consists of contaminated protective shoe covers and clothing, wiping rags, mops, filters, reactor water treatment residues, equipment and tools, luminous dials, medical swabs, injection needles, and syringes. The radioactivity can range from just above background levels found in nature to very high levels found in certain cases (such as parts from inside the reactor vessel in a nuclear power plant).

Package: the assembly of components and radioactive contents, as presented for transport, that is necessary to ensure compliance with the requirements of 10 CFR Part 71.

Performance-Based: an approach to regulatory practice that establishes performance and results as the primary bases for decisionmaking. Performance-based regulations have the following attributes: (1) measurable, calculable or objectively observable parameters exist or can be developed to monitor performance; (2) objective criteria exist or can be developed to assess performance; (3) licensees have flexibility to determine how to meet the established performance criteria in ways that will encourage and reward improved outcomes; and (4) a framework exists or can be developed in which the failure to meet a performance criterion, while undesirable, will not in and of itself constitute or result in an immediate safety concern.

Program Assessment Rating Tool: an instrument used by the Office of Management and Budget to inform budgeting decisions, support management, identify design problems, and promote performance measurement and accountability.

Regulatory Framework: several interrelated aspects such as (1) the NRC's mandate from the Congress in the form of enabling legislation, (2) the NRC's licenses, orders, and regulations in Title 10 of the *Code of Federal Regulations*, (3) regulatory guides, review plans, and other documents that clarify and guide the application of NRC requirements that amplify those regulations, (4) the licensing and inspection procedures used by NRC employees, and (5) enforcement guidance.

Risk Assessment: a systematic method for addressing the three questions as they relate to the performance of a particular system, including the human component—"What can go wrong?" "How likely is it?" and, "What are the consequences?"

Risk Insights: the results and findings that come from risk assessments. They may include improved understanding of the likelihood of possible outcomes, sensitivity of the results to key assumptions, relative importance of the various system components and their potential interactions, and the areas and magnitude of the uncertainties.

Risk-Informed: an approach to decisionmaking in which risk insights are considered along with other factors such as engineering judgment, safety limits, and redundant and/or diverse safety systems. Such an approach is used to establish requirements that better focus licensee and regulatory attention on design and operational issues commensurate with their importance to public health and safety.

Spent Fuel: fuel that has been removed from a nuclear reactor because it can no longer sustain power production for economic or other reasons.

Stakeholders: members of the public, Federal, State, local, and Tribal authorities, and licensees with a specific interest in a given topic.

Standards: technical requirements and recommended practices for the performance of any device, apparatus, system, or phenomenon associated with a specific field.

Yucca Mountain Repository: a proposed underground facility at Yucca Mountain, Nevada, for the permanent disposal of high-level waste produced from nuclear power plants and the Nation's nuclear weapons production activities.

Dry casks for spent fuel are transported and placed on a concrete pad at a nuclear plant site.

2. TITLE AND SUBTITLE	3. DATE REPORT PUBLISHED	
U.S. Nuclear Regulatory Commission Strategic Plan Fiscal Years 2008–2013	MONTH	YEAR
	February	2008
	4. FIN OR GRANT NUMBER	
	n/a	

5. AUTHOR(S)	6. TYPE OF REPORT	
Tammy Trocki, et. al	Triennial	
	7. PERIOD COVERED *(Inclusive Dates)*	
	Fiscal Years 2008—2013	

8. PERFORMING ORGANIZATION - NAME AND ADDRESS *(If NRC, provide Division, Office or Region, U.S. Nuclear Regulatory Commission, and mailing address; if contractor, provide name and mailing address.)*

Resource Management and Support Staff
Office of the Chief Financial Officer
U.S. Nuclear Regulatory Commission
Washington, DC 20555-0001

9. SPONSORING ORGANIZATION - NAME AND ADDRESS *(If NRC, type Same as above ; if contractor, provide NRC Division, Office or Region, U.S. Nuclear Regulatory Commission, and mailing address.)*

Same as 8, above

10. SUPPLEMENTARY NOTES

11. ABSTRACT *(200 words or less)*

The Strategic Plan Fiscal Years 2008–2013 descr bes the NRC's mission and establishes the Commission's strategic direction by defining the strategic goals and outcomes the agency intends to pursue.

12. KEY WORDS/DESCRIPTORS *(List words or phrases that will assist researchers in locating the report.)*	13. AVAILABILITY STATEMENT
Strategic Plan Fiscal Years 2008–2013 FY 2008–FY2013 Mission Goals Outcomes	unlimited
	14. SECURITY CLASSIFICATION
	(This Page)
	unclassified
	(This Report)
	unclassified
	15. NUMBER OF PAGES
	16. PRICE

NUREG-1614, Vol. 4

February 2008